Secrets of Mental Supremacy

W.R.C. Latson M.D

Alpha Editions

This edition published in 2019

ISBN : 9789353601584

Design and Setting By
Alpha Editions
email - alphaedis@gmail.com

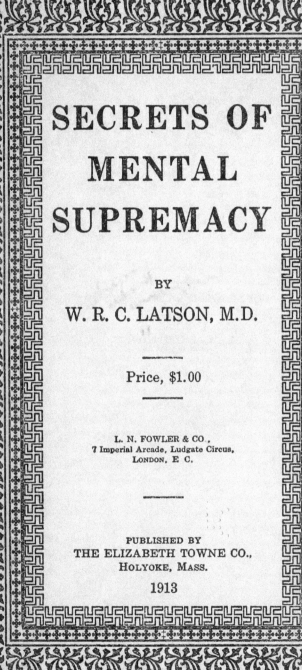

SECRETS OF MENTAL SUPREMACY

BY

W. R. C. LATSON, M.D.

Price, $1.00

L. N. FOWLER & CO.,
7 Imperial Arcade, Ludgate Circus,
LONDON, E C.

PUBLISHED BY
THE ELIZABETH TOWNE CO.,
HOLYOKE, MASS.
1913

CONTENTS.

My mind to me a kingdom is.—
  Epictetus.

The mind's the measure of the
  man.—*Watts.*

As a man thinketh in his heart,
  so is he.—*Jesus.*

The man does not contain the
  mind: the mind contains the
  man.—*Socrates.*

In the universe there is nothing
  great but man: in the man
  there is nothing great but
  mind.—*Aristotle.*

I.

INTRODUCTION.

N the brief articles which will make up this series my object will be to present in the shortest, plainest, and most practical manner methods which, in my experience and that of many others who have been more or less under my influence, have seemed to be conducive to increased mental efficiency.

It is said that there is no royal road to learning; and while in a sense this is true, it is also true that, in all things, even in mind training, there is a right way and a wrong way—or rather there is one right way, and there are a thousand wrong ways.

Now, after trying, it seems to me, most of the wrong ways, I have found what I believe to be the right way; and in these articles I shall try to expound it to you. You need not expect an essay on psychology or a series of dissertations upon the "faculties of the mind"; for there will be nothing of the kind. On the other hand, I shall, so far as possible, avoid text-book terms and the text-book tone—both of which are quite absurd and quite futile. I shall try to give you bare facts. I shall try to give you plain directions, stripped of all verbal and pseudo-scientific flummery, for the acquisition of mental activity and mental supremacy.

W. R. C. LATSON, M.D.

New York City.

II.

MIND AND ITS MATERIAL.

IRST of all, before you are able to think at all, you must have something to think about. You must have some mental "stock in trade." And this mental stock in trade you can gain only through the senses. The appearance of a tree, the roar of the ocean, the odor of a rose, the taste of an orange, the sensation you experience in handling a piece of satin—all these are so much material helping to form your stock of mental images—"the content of the consciousness," as the scholastic psychologists call it.

Now, all these millions and millions of facts which make up our mental stock in trade—the material of thought—are gained through the senses, sight, hearing, smell, taste, touch, and so on.

VALUE OF THE PERCEPTIONS.

In a recent article in a leading French scientific journal, a well-known scientist, Dr. A. Peres, has presented some ideas which are so thoroughly in accord with my own observations extending over many years, that I yield to the temptation to quote. Dr. Peres first makes note of modern degeneracy in this respect. I append a free translation of a few extracts which seem to me especially worthy of attention:—

" 'Have we naught but arms and legs? Have we not also eyes and ears? And are not these latter organs necessary to the use of the former? Exercise then not the muscles only, but the senses that control them.' Thus was a celebrated philosopher wont to express himself. Nevertheless when we measure acuteness of vision we find that it is becoming weaker; hardness of hearing is on the increase; we suffer daily from lack of skill in workmen, in domestics, in ourselves; as to taste and smell, they are used up—thus do the inevitable laws of atavism act.

"The trouble is that, despite Rousseau's objurgations, we have always paid too little attention to the hygiene and education of the senses, giving all our care to the development of physical strength and vigor; so that the general term 'physical education' finally has assumed the restricted meaning of 'muscular education.'

"The senses, which put us in contact with exterior objects, have nevertheless a primordial importance. . . . So great is their value that it is the interest and even the duty of man to preserve them as a treasure, and not to do anything which might derange their wonderful mechanism."

The length and exactness of the sight, the skill and sureness of the hand, the delicacy of the hearing, are

9

of value to artist and artisan alike by the perfection and rapidity of work that they insure. Nothing embarrasses a man so trained; he is, so to speak, ready for anything. His cultivated senses have become for him tools of universal use. The more perfect his sensations, the more justness and clearness do his ideas acquire. The education of the senses is the primary form of intellectual education.

"The influence of training on the senses is easily seen. The adroit marksman never misses his aim; the savage perceives and recognizes the slightest rustling; certain blind persons know colors by touch; the precision of jugglers is surprising; the gourmet recognizes the quality of a wine among a thousand others; odor is with chemists one of the most sensitive reactions.

"The senses operate in two ways, either passively, when the organ, solely from the fact that it is situated on the

10

surface of the body, and independently of the will, is acted upon by exterior bodies; or actively, when the organ, directed and excited by the will, goes, so to speak, in advance of the body to receive the impression. Passively, we see, hear, touch, smell; actively, we observe, listen, feel, sniff. By the effect of the attention and by arranging our organs in certain ways, our impressions become more intense. . . .

"The impressions made by exterior objects on the sense-organs, the nerves and the brain, are followed by certain mental operations. These two things are often confounded. We are in the habit of saying that our senses often deceive us; it would be more just to recognize that we do not always interpret correctly the data that they furnish us. The art of interpretation may be learned. . . .

"The intuitive, concrete form given nowadays to education contributes to the training of the senses by developing attention, the habit of observation; but this does not suffice. To perfect the senses and make each of them, in its own perceptions, acquire all possible force and precision, they must be subjected to special exercises, appropriate and graded. A new gymnastic must thus be created in all its details."

There are, of course, a certain number of "specific" or racial impressions and tendencies that come down through what is called heredity; but these are merely instincts and impulses, and while they have an influence upon the person's character and habits of thought, they do not, in themselves, provide actual material for thought.

If you can imagine a person who was blind and deaf, who could not smell or taste or feel or move; he would be quite unable to think, for he would have in his mind nothing about which to think. The material of thought, the mental stock in trade, is gained through the senses; and in any rational

12

effort to train the mind we must begin by training the senses—the perceptions, as they are more accurately called,—so that we may see, hear, smell, taste, and feel with more precision and keenness. Trained perceptions are the very foundation of all mental power.

Our system of training for mental supremacy will begin, then, with a brief study of the perceptions, or senses, and the methods by which we may gain the power of seeing more clearly, listening more intently, of feeling more delicately, and, in general, of developing the perceptive powers.

MEMORY AND ITS USES.

But the perceptions are of little value unless we remember what we have perceived. You may have read all the wise books ever written, you may have traveled the wide world over; you may have had all kinds of interesting and unusual experiences; but—unless you can remember what you have read, what you have seen, and what you have done —you will have no real use of it all. You will have gained no mental "stock in trade," no material by the employment of which you may hope to achieve mental supremacy. It will be necessary, then, for us to study not only methods of developing power of perception, but the means by which perception may be retained and recalled at will.

THE POWER OF ASSOCIATING MEMORIES.

But the memory itself is not enough. I have known people of unusual powers of memory who could not talk, write, or think well—who were like "the bookful blockhead, ignorantly read, with loads of learned humor in his head"; but who, in spite of all their experience and their recollection of it, had nothing to write, nothing to say.

So—memory is not enough. One

must have the power of putting memories together—of analyzing, comparing, contrasting, and associating memories—until the entire mass of memories, which form the "content of the consciousness," is wrought into one splendid, homogeneous whole—a mass of images, each one of which is intimately connected with many others, and all of which are under instant command of the central sovereign—the will.

It will be necessary, then, to give special attention to this most important matter of analyzing, comparing, and grouping mental images. Of all the activities of the mind this faculty, called "the power of association," is the one most directly conducive to what is generally called "a brilliant mind."

IMAGINATION AND JUDGMENT.

The possession of trained perceptions, of a retentive memory and great powers of association are of enormous

15

value; but only when combined with another faculty—imagination; and imagination is merely the power of recombining certain memories in such a fashion that the combination is new. Imagination is a faculty of the highest possible importance. Every splendid achievement, every invention, every business enterprise, every great poem, or book or picture, has been not only conceived but completed in imagination before it became actualized in fact.

And then it is necessary to be able to compare the mental pictures, gathered by the perceptions, remembered and classified by memory and association, so as to determine the relation of these memories to each other and their application to other ideas or mental images. And this valuable faculty of the mind is called judgment.

NECESSITY FOR CONCENTRATION.

Now, in order to do well in any one of the things of which I have been writing, it is necessary that the entire mind should be engaged upon that one thing. To do anything well one must do only that thing at that time. And this is particularly true of the action of the mind. The focusing of the entire power of the mind upon one thing is commonly known as concentration or "the power of attention."

So essential is this power of concentrating the entire mind upon the task in hand that it is not too much to say that no great degree of mental power can ever be gained without concentration. So in our study of the practical methods by which mental supremacy may be achieved, we shall pay special attention to the development of this invaluable faculty.

But in order to do anything with the mind (or with the body either, for that matter) one must choose, must wish to do that thing. And this choice, this decision to do something, is called the will. The power to choose quickly and decisively and to act vigorously upon that choice is a rather rare thing. He who has that power is said to have a strong will.

This question of will and its development is most important. The great difference between men — between strong men and weaklings, between the honored and the disregarded, between the masters and the serfs—is will. A man of strong, unfaltering will is sure to succeed even if his abilities are mediocre; but a man of weak will, no matter what his abilities, is not likely to achieve either success or honor among men.

As a great psychologist has said: "The education of the will is really of far greater importance than that of the intellect." And again: "Without this [will] there can be neither independence, nor firmness, nor individuality of character." Ik Marvel says: "Resolve is what makes a man manifest. . . . Will makes men giants."

18

The will, like any other mental faculty, may be highly developed by training; and this, with many practical exercises, also we will take up in its proper place.

IMPORTANCE OF THE SOCIAL FACULTIES.

The above brief outline of the mental powers embraces those which any one may develop and use without help from or association with other people. The highest powers of the mind, however, or at any rate, the most impressive powers of the mind, can be developed only through contact with others —through social intercourse.

A man might have miraculously keen perceptions, perfect memory, splendid imagination, infallible judgment, indomitable will—he might have all of these; and yet he would miss the rewards of mental supremacy unless he were capable of dealing with other people—unless he were socially accomplished.

In our efforts to train the powers of the mind, therefore, it will be necessary to make a study of some of the principles affecting our relations with other people; and so we shall in the same practical and straightforward way discuss sympathy, adaptability, and self-command. The important question of verbal expression as applied to both speech and writing will also receive special attention.

MENTAL ACTION A UNIT.

In conclusion you must not forget that, although I speak of the various mental acts as if they were separate, this is done only for convenience of discussion and description. As a matter of fact the mind is one thing—a unit. All the various "faculties" act together constantly. One cannot remember what an oak tree looks like unless he has carefully observed an oak tree. He cannot imagine an oak tree unless he remembers it. He cannot judge of the difference between an oak tree and a maple tree unless he can imagine a picture of the two side by side. And he cannot do any one of these things without attention; nor again can he concentrate his attention without an act of will.

So we see that the various acts of the mind, perception, memory, imagination, judgment, attention, and will, are inextricably interdependent—and that one act involves all the rest.

Happily this makes our task all the easier and more interesting. In this series I shall begin by giving you some plain practical advice as to the development of the perceptive powers—the ability to see, hear, feel, taste, and smell more efficiently. But with every moment of practice such as I advise you will also be developing a more exact and acute memory, a finer and more expansive imagination, a greater power concentration, and a stronger will. When we come to discuss the cultivation of the will power the exercises will require the use of the perceptions, the memory, the imagination, and other faculties. So, you see, in developing the mind in any one phase of its activity you are, at the same time and by the same act, adding to the power and usefulness of the entire mind.

III.

TRAINING OF THE PERCEPTIVE FACULTIES.

Man is the eyes of things.—HINDOO PROVERB.

HAT far-seeing genius, Goethe, once said that he regarded himself as the center of all phenomena, a sort of focus to which converged everything in the universe, out of which came—Goethe. He also claimed that the real standard for all things in life was simply the mass of sensations that were appreciable to the human senses.

In other words, Goethe understood perfectly the now widely recognized—and widely ignored—educational principle that all mental activity is based

23

upon the perceptions—upon the things we see and hear and feel and taste and smell.

As well might you try to build a house without wood or bricks or stone or mortar, as to try to think without a good "stock in trade" of impressions, images, and memories gathered by the senses and the perceptions.

BLURRED MENTAL PICTURES.

One of the never failing marks of the common mind, the untrained, inefficient mind, is that the mental pictures it contains are confused, blurred, inexact. A person with such a mind will tell you that an auto car just passed him on the road. "Was it a big, red car?" you ask. Well, he does not quite know. It might have been red, and yet he guesses it was black; possibly it was gray. How many people were in it? Three or four or five —four, he thinks. Ask him to give you an outline of a book he has read

24

or a play he has seen, and he is equally helpless. And so on.

Such a person is the typical inefficient. You will find thousands of these inefficients filling unimportant places in shops and offices. And even the trivial duties of such positions they are unable to perform properly. They cannot read a line of shorthand notes and be sure of its meaning; they cannot add a column of figures and be certain of the result without repeated checkings. Such unfortunates are the "flotsam and jetsam" of the commercial world—the unfit who, in the struggle for existence, must necessarily be crowded out by those whose mental processes are more positive and more exact.

The extent to which the perceptions can be developed is almost incredible. I know personally a bank teller who can detect a counterfeit coin without a glance at it, judging only by weight, feeling, and ring. Another man of my acquaintance makes a large salary merely by his ability to judge tea through its flavor—a "tea taster." I know an orchestra conductor who, in the full fortissimo of his sixty piece band, will detect a slight error of any one performer. I could give many other instances within my own experience of remarkable powers of trained perception.

THE PERCEPTIONS ARE EASILY TRAINED.

For the encouragement of those who are aware that they do not get the best possible service from their senses and perceptions—that they do not see all there is to be seen, hear exactly and distinctly and so on—for the benefit of these I may say at once that the senses and perceptions are easily trained. A month or two of discipline such as I am about to describe will show most marked and gratifying development. In most cases a few months' training is all that is necessary; for the habit of close observation is soon formed, and once formed no further thought is required. The matter takes care of itself.

THE PERCEPTIONS OF CHILDREN.

First of all, a word about the senses and perceptions of children. Just here is one of the grievous defects of our defective school system. It practically ignores the fact that the child develops, not through reasoning, but through observation and activity. The child observes everything. His senses are active and acute. Childhood is the time to accumulate observations and experiences; later they will form the material for thought and general development.

The child should be encouraged to perceive and to remember. All the methods which I am about to describe are applicable to children of less than ten years old. The more elaborate and far ranging the mass of perceptions are, memories which the child carries over from infancy and childhood into youth and adult age, the greater, other things being equal, will be his intellectual possibilities.

MOST OF US ARE SENSORILY STARVED.

Most of us are grossly deficient in mental images. At a test made not long ago in Boston eighty per cent. of the children had no idea what a beehive was like, over half of them had no conception of a sheep, and over nine tenths had no notion of the appearance or nature of growing wheat. Of course they knew of other things which the country bred child would not know; but fancy the loss in the imagination of one to whom the following lines arouse no vision of a pure, rustic matutinal scene:—

"The breezy call of incense-breathing morn,
   The swallow twittering from the straw-
      built shed,

28

The cock's shrill clarion or the echoing horn
No more shall rouse them from their lowly
bed."

THE GREAT SECRET OF SENSE TRAINING.

The great secret of a true development of the perceptions is discrimination—the realization of differences. To the savage a sound is a sound; to the musician it is excruciating discord or exquisite harmony. To the musician a little depression in the ground, a bent twig, a turned leaf—they are nothing; to the savage they mean food, an enemy, safety, or danger. In the printed pages the unlettered boor sees only foolish black marks on white paper; but in those black marks the man of education sees that which makes his heart beat faster, his eyes swim with tears—which tells him secrets of life the clodhopper will never, never know. The differences are in the trained or untrained perceptions.

Most of the exercises which I shall

describe are quite simple—many, perhaps, will seem trivial. But remember, as a great educator has said: "The . . . point in education is the power to attend to things which may be in themselves indifferent by arousing an artificial feeling of interest."

So the first exercise is quite simple—simple, but not easy. Try it and see.

Take any object you like—a book, a pen, a pair of scissors. Lay it on the table before you. Then take pencil and paper and describe it. Simply tell what you see. Can you? I doubt it. Tell its dimensions, weight, color, form, markings, lettering, origin, uses, possibilities, shortcomings. See how fully you can write about the object. The result will probably not please you. You will find that you have not nearly the powers of expression which you supposed you possessed. But—it is good training; and with practice your powers will grow rapidly.

30

You can do the same thing out of doors. Look at a mountain peak, the ocean, a horse, a bird. If you think for a moment there is nothing to write about these things read up "Poem in the Valley of Chamouni," Byron's splendid passage beginning "Roll on, thou deep and dark blue ocean, roll," the superb poem in the book of Job describing the horse, Shelley's "Skylark," and so on. James Whitcomb Riley has said: "There is ever a song somewhere, my child." And to find the material for the song it is necessary only to look with refined and educated perception—to look trying to see all the various sides, all the many phases of the object looked at. In the same way you should study also many other natural objects—autumnal tints, frost marks, snowflakes, trees, both their general form and the shape of their leaves, all the common flowers. Last of all, and in many respects most practically important of all, make it a habit to observe closely the human face. Try to recognize and discriminate the signs of education, refinement, intellect, in the face, as distinguished from the stigmata of ignorance, coarseness, and brutality.

Another good exercise for the training of the sight is this: Procure a number of ordinary marbles, say three dozen; one dozen each of red, of white, and of blue. Then mix them together in a receptacle. Now grasp a handful of the marbles, give one glance at them and throw them back again. Then note down how many of each color there were in the hand. At first you will find this difficult. In a short time, however, you will be able to distinguish at a glance between, say, three red, five white, and seven blue—and three red, six white, and six blue—with corresponding development of the powers of perception in all other directions.

A very simple and very good exer-

cise for the development of the faculty
of sight is the following:—

Procure about a dozen white pasteboard cards, say three by five inches
in size. Then with a small brush or
with a pen draw upon each a number
of small black circles. The circles
should be solid black, about one quar-
ter inch in diameter. On the first card
draw one, on the second two, and so on,
until the last, on which you will make
twelve. Group them so far as possible
in a circle.

Now to use them: Hold the cards
face downward and shuffle them.
Then take up the top one, give one
brief glance at it, and try to perceive
how many black circles there are upon
it. Don't try to count during your
brief glance. Don't squint, scowl, or
strain the eyes. Merely glance, and
then try to remember and count what
you saw. At first you will probably
find it difficult to discriminate between
five circles and six; after a time, how-

ever, you will be able to decide instantly upon any number of circles up to fifteen, twenty or even more.

TRAINING THE EAR TO HEAR.

Few people know how to hear. Of most it might well be said "ears and they hear not." I do not mean that in most people the organ of hearing is in any way defective, but that as a result of inattention and lack of practice they do not get clear, vivid impressions from the sounds which impinge upon their auditory apparatus.

One of the best methods of training the hearing faculty is to listen attentively to the varied sounds of the country. The humming of insects, the cry of the robin, thrush, catbird, blackbird, swallow,—all these and the many other sounds peculiar to the country should be carefully studied.

The sounds incidental to city life are less picturesque and in a sense less varied than those of the country; and yet, if we speak only of the musical advantages of the city, there alone we have material for a splendid auditory training. Concerts, the opera, social music, the phonograph, even the hand organs on the street provide opportunities for a training of the ear. These opportunities may be utilized in various ways. One of the best and most practical, perhaps, is to habitually require of one's self a knowledge of the melody of popular selections. How many people, not distinctly musical, know the air of the "Soldiers' Chorus" from "Faust," the "Toreador's Song" from "Carmen," or the overture to "Tannhauser"? And yet these are things that we hear every day on the street organs.

A very fine exercise for the development of the hearing faculty is merely to listen to the ticking of a watch. A method which I have found very practical and helpful is the following:—

Place the watch upon the table at

which you are sitting. Now turn toward it the left ear. Can you hear it? Yes, plainly. Move a foot, two feet, three, four, from the table. Can you hear the watch? Yes. Now increase the distance, foot by foot, until you can no longer hear the watch. Now listen! listen! Concentrating the attention upon the sound until, out of the silence, or of a confusion of sounds, there comes to you the clear, rhythmical ticking of the tiny mechanism. All this time you are sitting with your left ear turned toward the watch. The same practice should, of course, be gone through with the right ear.

This exercise is valuable not only in cultivating the power of hearing, but also in developing concentration of the attention and will. It is merely another phase of the same method by which an orchestra conductor can, at will, select one instrument out of a band, and hear only that one to the exclusion of any other piece.

TRAINING THE SENSE OF SMELL.

We hear much to the effect that, as an animal, man is inferior to the beasts of the field; but, like a great deal else that we hear, it is not true—at least not to any extent. The truth is that, merely as an animal, man is the masterpiece of creation. In actual strength, endurance, grace, and rapidity of motion, the best physical types of men compare favorably with any other animal of the same size and weight. This is a biological fact.

But in one respect, at least, he is distinctly inferior, and that is as regards the sense of smell. There are very few animals that are not better equipped than man in this respect. For this inferiority there are many reasons, which we cannot discuss in this place.

I may remark, however, that in some people the sense of smell is developed to a surprising degree. I once knew a woman, well born and highly educated who, while blindfolded, could name any one of her friends who came within a foot or two of her. The same woman was also usually able to determine, by their odor, the ownership of articles belonging to those whom she knew well. I know another woman who can distinguish copper, brass, steel, and iron by their taste and odor. I may also add that what we call "taste" is also largely smell. The achievements of tea, coffee, tobacco, and whisky experts depend very largely upon delicacy of the olfactory sense.

A good method of training this sense is the following: Procure a number of small pasteboard or wooden boxes such as are used by druggists in the dispensing of pills or tablets. Any druggist will provide them for a trifle. Then put into each box a small quantity of one of the following substances: cinnamon, cloves, red pepper, mustard, black pepper, ginger. A half dozen boxes are enough, selecting for them such of the above substances as are most readily procurable. To practice this method, simply close your eyes, open a box at random and try to determine what the substance is by the odor.

This method may be varied by having a number of small vials, each containing one of the fragrant oils, such as oil of cloves, wintergreen, lemon, verbena, lavender, peppermint, bergamot, nutmeg, and so on. It is a good plan also to take careful note of the distinctive odor of the various fragrant flowers so that they may afterward be recognized by the perfume which is peculiar to each.

TRAINING FOR THE TASTE.

There are, in reality, only four savors or tastes: sweet, sour, bitter, and salt. As I have just remarked, what we call taste is very largely smell, or flavor. The best way to develop delicacy of the gustatory sense is to eat very simple food, and to put thereon very little or no seasoning in the form of salt, sugar, mustard, pepper, vinegar, or other condiment. Then, and then only, will one be able to appreciate the real flavor of the food. No one, for instance, who is in the habit of using pepper and other condiments, can really taste a strawberry.

In conclusion, I want to emphasize two things: first, that a training of the perceptive powers is the best possible investment one can make—even regarding the matter from its lowest view point—the monetary; second, that the exercises which I have suggested in this chapter, while they may seem very simple, almost trivial, will in every case where they are seriously practiced, add immensely not only to the powers of perception but to practical efficiency of every faculty of the mind.

IV.

MEMORY AND HOW TO DE-VELOP IT.

Memory is accumulated genius.—
JAMES RUSSELL LOWELL.

*Memory is the permanence of per-ception.—*LATSON.

HE value of any man to himself and to the world at large depends in great degree upon his mem-ory—upon his ability to recall and to use at any desired moment the recollection of what he has seen, heard, experienced, or thought.

Memory is really the stock in trade of our mental life. Our perceptions bring to us a vast mass of experiences—things that we have seen, heard, touched, tasted, and smelled—our thoughts and

41

experiences. But these things are valuable only when they are held in the memory. For, unless they are remembered they cannot be used. Most of us have forgotten much more than we remember. We have studied — at school, at college, at home. We have read many, many books. We have had any number of interesting and instructive conversations. We have, some of us, traveled and seen many rare and curious things. And of it all, how much is in our possession at the moment—how much is at our ready command? Not one tenth—probably not one hundredth.

Imagine the enormous loss to us. Imagine the waste of time and effort. Imagine what it would mean to you or to me if, instead of possessing a memory which preserved for us only one hundredth of our experiences, we could remember and apply at will one half, three quarters, four fifths of what we have been through.

MENTAL SUPREMACY.

"But that is impossible," you say.
Allow me to contradict you. There have
been many cases of recollective power
which prove otherwise. The most
striking of these was Antonio Magliabecchi, who lived in Italy in the sev-
enteenth century. From being a mere
servant he rose until he became the
librarian of Cosmo III., the Grand
Duke of Turin. Magliabecchi's memory was prodigious; nothing that he
had ever seen or heard or experienced
was ever lost to him. It is said that
after one reading he could repeat verbatim any book in the library of his
patron, who at this time owned one of
the largest collections of the day.

"Impossible," you say. Not at all.
I know a man who can neither read
nor write except to sign his name. He
is an Irishman who began life in this
country with a pick and a shovel. To-
day he is a man of wealth and power,
financially and politically. He is a
contractor, real estate operator, stock

43

speculator, and is interested in several other lines of business. He keeps no books and employs no bookkeepers. All his values, dates, and figures are carried in his head; and at any moment he can tell to a cent how he stands with any of his business associates.

Among the ancient Greeks it was not at all unusual to find an educated patrician who could recite verbatim the entire poems of Homer—the Iliad and the Odyssey. Cyrus the Great could call by name any man of his army, numbering one million. Napoleon had power of memory almost as remarkable. Gladstone, when presenting to Parliament his yearly budget, would speak for several hours, presenting monetary details running into many million pounds without one glance at the written report lying on the table before him. Robert G. Ingersoll, that great jurist and brilliant orator, would attend a trial lasting many days without taking any notes. Yet

in his speeches to the jury, lasting
sometimes many hours, he never for-
got or missed a point of the oppo-
sition.

And so I might go on. Scott, Milton,
Shakespeare, Washington, Clay, Web-
ster—all these were remarkable for
their power of memory. In fact it is
safe to say that every man who has ever
attained a high place among men has
been possessed of a retentive and exact
memory.

So we can see that, as an asset in
practical life, whether one's ambition
be literary, artistic, scientific, or
merely the transferring of dollars from
some one's pocket into his own—as a
practical asset, power of memory is of
the highest conceivable value. A good
memory will give you an incalculable
advantage over others—an advantage
which no other mental qualification
will balance.

MEMORY TRAINING NOT DIFFICULT.

The mind is like potter's clay—it is easily molded. And there is no direction in which development is so easy as in the department of memory. Even a few days of practice along the lines which I shall suggest will generally make a noticeable difference, and two or three months of conscientious training will often be sufficient to metamorphose a poor, weak, and inexact memory into one that is tenacious and reliable.

THE NATURE OF MEMORY.

In the introductory article of this series I promised you that I would not be theoretical or descriptive, but that I would make these chapters purely practical. Now, I intend to keep my word; but, in order to make what follows more intelligible and helpful, it will be well just here to stop for a moment and make a few brief statements as to the nature of memory.

In the first place, I may say at once

that, in reality, there is no such thing
as "the memory." This sounds very
much like an old-fashioned Irish
"bull"; but it is merely a statement of
sober fact. There is no memory: there
are only memories. When I say that
I am not merely juggling with terms;
the difference is important and funda-
mental.

I mean just this: Memory is not,
as we used to be taught many years
ago, a "faculty of the soul"—a little
section of the brain to be developed all
by itself. Not at all. Memory is
merely a term used to describe the way
that certain acts or thoughts tend to
remain in the mind. And every act
or thought has its own separate little
memory.

Some acts or thoughts we remember
easily; other acts or thoughts we remember with difficulty, if at all. If
some one were to describe to me the
details of a case of insanity, symptoms,
history, treatment, I should remember

it a long time; because, as a physician, I am interested in psychiatry. But, although I listened patiently a day or two ago to a long account of the Wall Street adventures of an acquaintance of mine, I am quite sure that I could give no intelligent account thereof, because I know little and care less about such matters. In the same way some people have good memory for names, but cannot recall faces, others can remember dates, but have no power to recollect names. And so on.

The point is just this: We remember best the things in which we have most interest, the things with which we are most familiar. The little memory of any act or thought may stick in the mind or it may not—whether it is or is not remembered depends mainly upon the amount of attention we have given to that act or that thought at the time it was occurring.

If, therefore, we would have fine powers of memory—if we desire a

large supply of clear, vivid memories
all under instant command, it is essential that we should pay to the thing
we wish to remember strict attention
and careful study. And this is really
the great secret of what is called "good
memory."

In other words, a memory is simply
a permanency, a recurrence, of a perception; and that memory is clear and
complete just in proportion as the perception was clear and complete. If,
on an introduction to a stranger, I
scarcely glance at his face and pay
little or no attention to the name, I am
not likely to remember either the man
or the name. If, on the other hand,
I look closely at him and attend carefully to the name, I shall be likely to
remember it, perhaps for years.

I, myself, frequently have presented
to me twenty-five or thirty strangers
in the course of an evening; and I am
usually able afterward to recall all or
nearly all of their names and faces.

This is merely the result of a habit of attention to the matter.

THE BASIC LAW OF MEMORY.

Now, then, based upon the principle just discussed, we may formulate our first rule for the development of memory: Study the object you wish to remember in all its phases, in all its peculiarities, in all its relations. For the time being keep every other thought out of the mind. Make the object part of yourself; and you will never forget it. I say object, but I mean, of course, anything, fact, figure, idea, principle, or plan, to all of which the same rule applies.

So much for the rule; but you would like to know exactly how to apply this rule to practical development. Well, one of the best ways I know is the following:—

You are walking down the street. A carriage passes at which you have glanced casually. After it has passed, question yourself about it. What kind of a carriage was it—landeau, barouche, brougham, or what? What was the color of the wheels? Had they rubber tires? How many horses were there? Their color? The coachman—black or white? The livery, if any? How many occupants—men or women? How dressed? Do you remember all their faces, so that if you saw them again you would know them? And so on.

By the time you have done this conscientiously on a dozen occasions you will be surprised and delighted at the improvement in your ability both to perceive and to remember; for, as I cannot reiterate too often, the two, perception and memory, are practically one.

Well, after passing the carriage and getting all the good you can out of the experience in an educational way, you will come to a shop window—the window of a toy shop, let us say. Don't stop to look at the window; that will merely confuse you. Take one glance at it, and pass on.

Then ask yourself what you saw in the window. If practicable have a pad and pencil, and write down each article as you remember it. This is the method employed by the famous conjurer, Robert Houdin—a method by which he so trained the memory both of himself and of his young son that they were able to remember over thirty thousand questions and answers, which formed the code of their famous "second sight" act.

Another valuable method of memory training is to make it a rule every night, either before or after retiring, to review in detail the events of the day. This was the method employed by the great Edward Thurlow, lord high chancellor of Great Britain. At first his memory was so poor that he was unable to recall what he had eaten for breakfast. Eventually, however, he developed one of the most remarkable memories on record. I know of a number of cases in which this method has proven of the utmost value.

Another very simple and convenient, but at the same time very useful, method of culturing the power of recollection is the following: Take some interesting book, such as a historical work, or some attractive novel. Read a paragraph to yourself slowly and carefully. Then close the book and repeat aloud the substance of the section which you have just read. Make no attempt to repeat the passage word for word. Simply give the sense of it as you remember. It matters little whether you repeat the author's words or use your own. After your first attempt (which is not likely to be a striking success) read the paragraph again and make a second effort to recall and express its general meaning.

When you have learned this paragraph fairly well, pass on to the next, and so on, until you come to the last paragraph on the page. Then take that page as your task, and give an account of the entire page. After practicing this way on every paragraph and every page until the end of the chapter, take the chapter as a whole and repeat it as fully and exactly as you can.

This seems like hard work. And it is, at first. But it soon becomes interesting, especially as you begin to find that, although at first you were unable to give any clear idea of a paragraph you had just read, you are soon able to recall, and to clearly express, the sense of an entire chapter without any great effort or difficulty.

This exercise trains not only the memory, but the perceptions, the will, and the powers of expression. So far as I know, it was invented by Henry Clay, in his early farm boy days, and was often quoted by him as being the method which had done most toward developing his prodigious memory and splendid oratorical ability.

A valuable variation of the above exercise is to write out at length, instead of attempting to express in spoken words, your recollection of the paragraph, the page, the chapter. For those who desire the widest development—a development of the power of expression in writing as well as in speech—I should suggest that they practice this exercise by both talking and writing their memories of the passage.

By the time you have gone over one book in this way, talking out certain passages and writing others, you will not only know that book in a way that few people ever know any book; but you will have developed added powers of attention, will power, memory, and expression, which will prove a surprise and a delight to you.

The Pictorial Faculty.

One of the prime secrets of memory is to develop the ability to recall before the mind a picture of the object desired —a vivid recollection of its appearance. When a schoolboy I discovered that there was no use whatever in my studying either my spelling or my geography lesson. All that was necessary was for me to pass my eye slowly down the list of words for spelling and to look at the map of the particular section we were studying. After that I could bring up before me a clear picture of any word called for or of any section of the map covering our lesson. In questioning musicians who are able to play from memory long passages on the piano or violin, I find that in the majority of cases they remember the appearance of the page of music, and follow the notes just as if the real page were before them. This power of visualizing memories has been in some people developed to a surprising extent. The mnemosynic achievements of the Houdins and of Magliabecchi referred to above, as well as of other prodigies like the mathematical wonder, Zerah Colburn, and his prototype, Jacques Inaudie—the memory feats of these depend largely, in some cases entirely, upon the visualizing faculty.

And what is the best method of developing this power of sight memory? There are several very simple and valuable. First try this: Write out in a clear hand a list of words in column form. The list should contain at first not more than five or six words; later it may be extended to twenty or even thirty.

Now place your list of six words before you and look at it for a moment. Don't stare or strain the eyes. Don't try to remember the words—yet. This is the moment for observation—for getting upon the photographic plate of the mind a clear memory-picture of the list of words. After a moment of steady gazing, cover the paper and try to remember exactly what the words were and how they looked. At first you are likely to find this difficult. Soon it will be easy to remember six— to recall the words, passing up as well as down the column. Then gradually increase the number until you can handle at least twenty-five.

A useful variation of this exercise is to use figures instead of words, arranging them at first as a square of four figures, and calling each one off while you remember its position. Here again, as soon as four is easy for you, increase the number of figures by two, until you can retain, after a single look, a clear picture of thirty-six or more figures. I have known a boy of twelve who was able to remember sixty-four figures—a square of eight figures up and eight across. He would, on request, call off first line of figures forward, third line of figures backward, line of units down, and so on—in other words, this boy could see in his mind's eye a mental picture of those sixty-four figures that was absolutely as clear as the original had been to the physical eye.

I may add that the boy I refer to was not in any sense exceptional, save that he had become interested in the "tricks" which I taught him and his fellows. All of them are now men of notably fine memory.

The same method may be varied in other ways. For instance, letters may be substituted for the figures or words may be arranged in groups, say twelve in groups of three each, the exercise being to remember not only the word but its position in relation to the other words. So exercises for developing the power of memory can be multiplied indefinitely. Those given above, however, are more than sufficient, if properly practiced.

Union accomplishes all things.—
SOPHOCLES.

*I have only to take up this or that to flood my soul with memories.—*MME. DELUZY.

*The whole art of mental training is based upon the fact that any action at first executed with conscious effort becomes, in time, sub-conscious and habitual.—*THOMPSON JAY HUDSON.

Within the secret chambers of the
      brain,
The thoughts lie linked by many a
      mystic chain.
Awake but one, and lo, what legions
      rise!
Each stamps its image as the other
      dies.

          —COWPER.

V.

ASSOCIATION OF IDEAS.

F all the operations of the mind the one most directly conducive to mental readiness is the power of associating or grouping ideas. The man or woman in whom the power of association is well developed has a mind which may be likened to a vast skein of threads. Each thread represents an idea. And of these thread-ideas all those which are at all related are grouped together like so many threads tied in a knot; so that if you touch one of the thread-ideas you are instantly in communication with all of that group.

When ideas are grouped or associated in this orderly manner any thought coming into the mind will instantly suggest a large number of related thoughts. This means an active, an efficient, frequently a brilliant mind.

Now let us understand at once that what is commonly called "education" —that is, a mere knowledge of facts— no matter how extensive it may be, does not necessarily confer the power of associating or grouping ideas in such a manner that they are readily available for purposes of speaking, writing, or thinking. Indeed I have known men of vast learning who could not talk well, who could not write well, who could not even think well. A well stored mind—that is, mere erudition, while it can be acquired only by a person with a good memory, does not by any means necessarily imply the power of association.

One who possesses unusual power of associating ideas is always interesting; often brilliant. His ideas are, as I have said, like threads knotted together. Each idea suggested to him calls up in his mind many related ideas.

In the mind of the merely erudite man, for instance, the mention of the word "horse" will arouse few, if any, other mental pictures. In the mind, however, of the person who has the power of association the idea "horse" awakens a large number of interesting thoughts. There is the horse so superbly described in the biblical poem, Job. There is the famous horse Bucephalus, the war charger of Alexander the Great, whom only he could ride. The person with strong power of association remembers, too, the wonderful horse, Kantara, ridden by Gautama, the Buddha. Then he thinks of the horse of Darius which, by neighing at the critical moment, caused his master to be elected king of Persia—Darius the Great. He recalls to mind the story of the great wooden horse, inside of which the Greek soldiers were smuggled into Troy, to the downfall of that city. And lastly, the man with trained powers of association will be able to tell you something about the interesting history of the horse, both before and since it was first tamed and ridden many thousands of years ago by Melizeus, King of Thessaly.

And so with any other subject you might suggest to him. In the mind of such a person every idea is intimately associated with many other more or less related ideas; and, even though his actual stock of information may be small, his mental images are so closely connected and so quickly recalled that the practical power and usefulness of his mind is greater than in the case of another person with a larger stock of knowledge and inferior power of association.

Another great advantage of well-developed powers of association is that it is almost a preventive of forgetfulness. As I have explained in the chapter on the training of the memory, that which we fully understand, we do not, cannot, forget. Now a complete understanding of any idea is simply the result of a process of making that idea the center of a mass of associations.

If you had to leave your boat in a stream with a very rapid current you would tie the boat to the shores, not only with one rope but with several ropes running to different points on each side of the stream. And the more lines you tie the boat with and the more directions they extend in, the less likely will your boat be to escape, and the more readily can you recover it at will. The same principle applies to ideas. Each associational relation is like a tiny thread binding one particular idea to another idea; and, when we bind that one particular idea to a great many other ideas, we make sure, first, that we will not forget it, and second, that when there comes into the mind any one of the ideas with which we have associated the new idea, the new idea will immediately be drawn into the mind.

All this being true, we will be ready to appreciate the following important statement: It is necessary to get into the mind a large stock of ideas; this can be done only by perception and memory; but it is equally necessary that the ideas and memories in the mind shall be so associated or grouped that one idea instantly calls up many other related ideas. And this can be done only by developing the power of association.

HOW ASSOCIATIONS ARE MADE.

And here arises the practical question: How shall I so train my mind that the ideas it contains shall be closely associated, each one with many others?

In trying to give you an intelligible answer to this question it will first be necessary to discuss briefly something of the process by which associations are formed in the mind.

Some one has said: "Thoughts are things." Now this statement is quite meaningless unless we have a clear idea as to what is meant by the term "thing." But let us imagine for a moment that the "thing" is something concrete, commonplace, and physical, like a brick—an ordinary building brick. For a thought may be regarded as an object, a thing, just as a brick can be studied as an object, a thing.

Now in order to make associations around anything we must first of all get a clear idea of that thing. And so we must begin by studying our brick— analyzing it. We will find that the brick has form, color, dimensions (length, breadth, thickness), weight, hardness, roughness, certain utilities and possibilities, history, money value, and so on. This process of determining the qualities peculiar to the object or idea is called analysis; and analysis

is the first step essential to the forma-
tion of associations. For it should be
understood that most of the ideas associated with any particular object are
based, not upon that object as a whole,
but upon some quality or qualities of
the object.

Now having analyzed our brick we
may take certain of its qualities and
on that basis make associations between the brick and other objects or
ideas. If we take its form we shall find
that it is something like a wooden pav-
ing block, something like a book, something like a cigar box. If we take the
usual color of the brick-red, we note
that it resembles terra cotta, the building material, that it is a shade frequently seen in wall covering and rugs
and also found in the shingle stains
often used on the roofs of country
houses. As to the uses of the brick,
we find the brick can be associated with
granite, marble, and other building
materials, cobble stones, wooden pav-

ing blocks, concrete, and various other substances used for pavement, and so on.

Now, in all this we have gone through four distinct processes of reasoning; and, without these four processes, no association between ideas could exist. First of all we analyzed our brick; next we extended our ideas of it, trying here and there until we found certain objects which could be associated with the brick. Lastly we noted that every other object we thought of was either like the brick in some certain particular or was entirely unlike it in every particular. These processes we may call extension, likeness, and unlikeness.

So these four processes of reasoning —analysis, extension, likeness, and unlikeness—must be gone through in order to make complete and valuable associations.

In the example just given I chose for my object a brick because the mere fact of its being a simple, prosaic, and commonplace object rendered my explanation more clear. The same process, the same treatment, however, may and, in fact, must be applied to other and more complicated ideas.

First of all we analyze the object from every standpoint and in every particular and detail. If a concrete object we study all its qualities as we did in the case of the brick. If an idea, we consider carefully all its phases. Then trace all its relations to other ideas, noting in what respect it resembles or differs from such other ideas. Then we shall have gone through the four processes—analysis, extension, likeness, and unlikeness.

To give you an instance illustrating this interesting and important method: Not long ago I was one of a number of guests at a country house. One evening when a number of us were sitting on the porch, the little daughter of our hostess approached with a dish

containing some fine apples, and said
to me: "Will you have an apple, Doc-
tor?" "My dear, that is a dangerous
question to ask a man," said I. "Do
you not know that all the sin and misery in the world came because a woman
once asked a man to have an apple—
and because he took it?"

And the child laughed and said:
"Oh, I know. You mean the apple that
Adam took from Eve." Clever child!

Now my remark was made without
any conscious effort of mind whatever
—without any striving or deliberate
action of the will. It was entirely sub-
conscious and effortless. Afterward I
amused myself by tracing out exactly
what my mind had done when the child
asked that question. And this is what
happened: Analysis "girl—offers apple." Out of this analysis I selected the
idea "apple" and upon this based my extension. First of all I thought of the old
adage "tender as the apple of the eye."
Then in rapid succession there came

into my mind memories of: the apple that William Tell is said to have shot off the head of his son; "apples of gold in pitchers of silver" mentioned in the Bible; the "apple of Sodom," the fruit of the osher tree, which is beautiful externally but filled with a kind of ashes—therefore often used as a symbol for disappointment; the apples of the Hesperian field, said to be guarded by the four mystic sisters—the Hesperides; the apple for which Paris ran his race.

Now all of these ideas, found by extension of the original idea "apple," were appropriate; but none seemed quite to fit. Then came the thought of the story of Eve and her proffer of the "apple" to Adam. This exactly fitted the occasion. And hence the reply.

In this instance also you can easily trace the processes—analysis, extension, seeking resemblances or likenesses, and discarding ideas less appropriate or unlike. And do not forget that, in the mind that is even fairly well trained, these pictures flash up with incredible rapidity. I know that in my own mind, as in the instance just cited, six or seven pictures will often occur, and I will select the one which it seems appropriate to mention, within the few seconds that ordinarily intervene between a remark and the reply to it.

ASSOCIATION AND MEMORY.

In an earlier paragraph I told you that proper association of ideas practically insured power of memory. Let me now try to give you some notion of how this principle of mental activity can be utilized.

Let us take a simple instance. Epictetus says: "My mind to me a kingdom is." Now, first of all, we consider this splendid utterance until we thoroughly understand and appreciate it. That is good, but it is not enough. We desire to possess this sentence—to make it a part of our mental stock in trade, so that we can use it at appropriate times in public speaking, in writing or in conversation. How shall we do this? Well, we have really four ideas in the quotation: the mind, a kingdom, contentment (implied), and the personality of the man, Epictetus, who wrote the sentence.

Let us first learn something of Epictetus. Let us analyze his character and place a mental picture of him in the midst of a network of associations which will make that picture of Epictetus our own forever. We find the following points for association: A slave—became free—great philosopher —blameless life—banished—friend of Adrian and Marcus Aurelius.

So we may associate the picture of Epictetus with the following ideas: slaves who were great men; great philosophers who were banished; men of humble origin who became friends of kings; Adrian and Marcus Aurelius—

any one of these will almost certainly suggest to us the idea, the mental picture, of Epictetus.

Now to return to Epictetus' sentence: The three ideas, kingdom, mind, contentment, should each be dwelt on for a moment in this wise: Kingdom, a place of vast extent, unlimited resources, boundless possibilities, infinite powers, much to explore, much to conquer. And to Epictetus, his mind was like a kingdom; and he was content. After the idea of a kingdom of great extent, take up the thought of the mind and its possibilities. Dwell on this until you see how, to a man of intellect, the mind is really a kingdom—a kingdom more interesting and wonderful than any mere physical country could possibly be. Then ponder on the notion of contentment in spite of humble circumstances. Associate this with the idea of Thoreau, of Purun Dass, of Diogenes, of Gautama, and of Jesus of Nazareth—

all of whom were content to live simply, finding their kingdom in the mind and soul. "My kingdom is not of this world," said Jesus.

Thereafter any of these ideas will be likely to suggest the epigram we are studying; for all of these ideas are now united together by the network of associations we have constructed.

Now to work out in this way all the many things which you want to remember and to have at instant command, seems, of course, like very hard work. Happily, however, such a method of forming associations, of binding ideas into bundles or clusters, as it were, is necessary only until the habit is once formed. Then the matter goes on automatically, of itself.

CONSCIOUS ACTION BECOMES UNCONSCIOUS.

It is a beneficent law of the mind (and of the body, too, for that matter) that any act, after it has been repeated a certain number of times, tends to become automatic—to do itself without any sensation of effort, sometimes even without our knowledge. A few months of careful effort will in practically every case develop such a habit of associating apposite ideas, that the student will possess, without further care or drill, this most superb accomplishment of the mind—the power of association.

It requires both care and attention to form any desirable habit, either of mind or body; but, the habit once formed, no further care or attention is necessary. To learn to write, for instance, to form the letters, to combine them into words, to elaborate the words into sentences and paragraphs, the paragraphs into pages—all this takes time, a number of years. Once thoroughly learned, however, as by a trained writer, the practice of writing requires no special care or effort.

And so with this important matter of association. Few people have it to any great degree. In most people the ideas are separate, isolated. Cardinal Newman says of some seafaring men that they "find themselves now in Europe, now in Asia; they see visions of great cities and wild regions; they are in the marts of commerce or in the islands of the south; they gaze on Pompey's Pillar or on the Andes; and nothing which meets them carries them forward or backward to any idea beyond itself. Nothing has . . . any relations; nothing has a history or a promise." All this means, in a word, that these men have not the power of association.

In order to arrange our ideas into clusters or groups, we must for a time give special attention to the matter. As a help to study along these lines, I can recommend the following exercises which have proven in my own personal experience and in that of others advised by me, of the greatest possible value.

Take any object you like—a rose, a pencil, a chair, a wheel, a knife. Having selected your object write out a list of its peculiarities. Say you have taken a knife—an ordinary table knife. Now, describe its form, color, size, shape, weight, material, and state its peculiarities—hard, cool, sharp, heavy, opaque, elastic.

Having written out this list of descriptive points, take them up one by one and think of what other objects have the same quality. For instance, in material the knife, being of steel with an ivory handle, resembles all cutlery and steel machinery, differing from them not in material but perhaps in the manner and degree of the tempering. The ivory handle will suggest a large number of articles made of that material. The sharpness of the knife suggests lancets, swords, scissors, and so on, and may also be applied in a figurative way, as to the nature of a remark ("Her words were

like a dagger thrust into his soul");
or the effect of a glance ("An eye like
a bayonet thrust met mine") and so on.
This treatment of the object "knife"
if done exhaustively will prove a most
valuable exercise. Three or four hours
over it will be time well spent. Not
that you are specially interested in the
subject "knife," its analysis or its relations, but that in going through the
exercises with any object whatever,
you are getting your mind into the
habit of treating all subjects in the
same analytical manner. By the time
you have treated twenty different objects in accordance with this method,
you will have gone far toward gaining
the invaluable accomplishment of associating ideas.

VI.

IMAGINATION AND HOW TO CULTIVATE IT.

The mind can make substance and people planets of its own.—BYRON.

The universe to man is but a projection of his own inner consciousness.—KANT.

F all the powers of the mind, imagination is the most picturesque, and, in many respects, the most interesting. Without it the world would be barren. Not merely would there be no pictures, no music, no books, but there would be no houses, no bridges, no ocean greyhounds, no great business enterprises — nothing, in fact; for everything that man has made has been first conceived in the imagina-

tion before it was born into actual being.

We cannot think of a person being without any power of imagination; for that is an impossibility. But many, many people, I am sorry to say, are greatly deficient in imagination; and this lack of imagination alone is enough to render them commonplace, uninteresting, and of little use or significance in the world.

A man or woman may be deficient in imagination and yet be honest, straightforward, hard working, conscientious. But for such a man or such a woman the higher rewards of life are hopelessly unattainable. He or she may make an excellent bookkeeper, but never an accountant; a skillful typist, but never a secretary; a faithful stockboy, but never a salesman. The accountant, the secretary, the salesman, must have imagination.

Of course when it comes to any actual creative work—painting, sculpture, musical composition, literature—the power of imagination, highly trained, refined, daring, and vivid, is the great essential. The creators of famous masterpieces have, in instances, lacked everything else but this one thing—imagination. Some of the great artists have lived all their lives in misery and want. Some have been ignorant, some have been coarse, some have been immoral, some have been eccentric, some have been almost or quite insane. But one thing all have possessed in common, and that is—a superb imagination.

In no respect, I believe, do men differ so widely as in the power and activity of their faculty of imagination. Hundreds of men and women have walked and sat in the old country churchyard, and no one had observed there anything that was especially interesting or picturesque. But one day there came to the churchyard a man with a fine imagination, a poet. He saw more than mere grass and trees and headstones; and he gave to the world the most perfect poem in the English language. His name was Thomas Gray, and the poem was the famous "Elegy in a Country Churchyard."

Thousands of people had seen an apple fall from a tree to the ground. But one day a man with a great imagination saw that commonplace thing. His imagination seized upon it, and he propounded Newton's theory of the law of gravitation, one of the most important achievements in the whole history of human thought. Another man sees his mother's teakettle boiling. He observes that the lid is raised by the expanding steam. His great imagination starts from this homely detail; and he gives to the world—the steam engine. Napoleon, poor, obscure, hungry, trudging up and down the streets of Paris in search of employment, dreams of making all Europe one vast empire—his empire. And he all but succeeds.

And so we might go on indefinitely. Enough, perhaps, to repeat that the world's masters have always been possessed of fine and daring imagination, and that, without great powers of imagination, there can be accomplished no great or important work of any nature whatever.

IMAGINATION EASILY CULTIVATED.

Perhaps you feel that your own imagination does not always serve you as well as it should; perhaps you are wishing that it was better—that you could produce in it such improvement as to enable you to create some good and worthy thing in the world. In that case I am glad to be able to tell you that, of all the powers of the mind, none is capable of being so easily, conveniently, and rapidly cultivated as the imagination. And I may remark that, as in the case of other faculties, the means taken to cultivate the imagination will at the same time necessarily train and strengthen the mentality in every other direction.

First of all, it must be understood that the act of imagining, of bringing images before the mind, is not a separate function of the mentality, but that it is closely interwoven with, partly consists of, in fact, several other of the mental faculties. So in developing the power of imagination we must first speak of these other faculties which are really a part of it. If we study an act of imagination, we shall find that first of all we must have some material for our image.

To most people the act of imagination means the creation of something entirely new. They think that the picture created by the painter, the poet, the novelist, is new in every detail. Now, this is a radical error. The artist does not create anything that is entirely new. And this for a very good reason—there is not and never will be anything entirely new. Now, as in the days of Solomon: "There is nothing new under the sun."

You may imagine, for instance, a green horse with purple wings. You say: Surely, that is an entirely new idea. I say: No, it is merely a new combination of four very old and commonplace ideas—a horse, a pair of wings, and the two colors, green and purple. And so in all creations, no matter what they may be —however new they may seem—it is only the combination that is new. The materials combined are old, as old, very often, as human thought itself.

We see, then, that the first raw material for imagination is our percepts—the things we have seen and heard and felt and smelled and tasted. And it seems hardly necessary to state that the better service we have gotten from our senses and perceptions, the more clear and vivid will be our power to bring before the mind images made up of those things. The first task, then, of him who would develop his power of imagination is to educate the senses.

IMAGINATION AND MEMORY.

But the imagination requires more than mere perception. The things perceived must be remembered. A thing that we have forgotten—lost out of the conscious mind—cannot be used as material for an act of imagination. And then the things perceived and remembered should have been grouped and associated into clusters; so that when one wishes to imagine a certain picture he will have a vast amount of material in his mind from which to select materials for that picture.

In cultivating the power of imagination, then, we must begin by educating perception, memory, and association; for (and here is my definition of imagination) imagination is merely a combination of perception, memory, and association with initiative, will. This is not at all text-bookish; but it will give you—as the text-books probably would not on such short acquaintance —a clear idea of the process.

SOME PRACTICAL EXERCISES.

Let me state right here that you are exercising your imagination all the time during all your waking hours. You imagine thousands of things every day. Everything you do, every person you go to meet, everything you say— these are all in the imagination before they become realities. Your imagination has much exercise, but—it is not the right kind of exercise. The mental pictures are not clear and vivid. How shall you make them so? Demand it of yourself. And this brings me to your first practical exercise.

Get a good, lively novel, something full of action, and as near as possible to the here and the now. Make yourself comfortable and begin to read. When you come to the end of the first paragraph, stop and image before your mind a clear picture of what was expressed or described. Was it a scene? See it, mountains, sea, farmhouse, city residence, cold, warm, rainy, bright. Try to make it as vivid as it would be were you actually gazing on the scene. That is what the writer of the story did, or you would not be reading it. During the next paragraph the scene is changed; something is added to the picture. See this. Take much time; it is an exercise. Then comes a person, say a man. See him. Is he tall, short, dark, light, prepossessing, repellent? How is he dressed? Force yourself to imagine every detail. And so on, for a chapter.

By this time you will have had enough for once; but if you have acted conscientiously in accordance with my hints, you will feel an understanding, an interest, and a sympathy with that book and its characters that will surprise you. By the time you have read a dozen chapters in this manner you will have proven to yourself in many ways that your imagination—and, in fact, all your mental powers—have markedly improved. Besides, you will know for the first time the real joy of reading. This is the kind of reading Emerson had in mind when he said: "There is the creative reading as well as creative writing."

Another method by which the imaging faculty can be cultivated is the following: Take fifteen or twenty minutes at the end of the day and make a detailed review of its more important occurrences. Take much time; supply every detail; see and hear again everything that was said and done. Examine each episode critically. What mistakes did you make? In what way could you have handled the situation more easily, advantageously, diplomatically? How would you proceed again under similar circumstances? In this exercise be careful, first, to see— actually see, clearly and vividly—every event, person, action, detail, of each episode; second, in imagining how you, yourself, and others might have acted, beware of criticising the actions of other people. Try to feel that whatever went wrong, you, yourself, had you possessed sufficient will, sympathy, delicacy, intelligence, and control might have made it right. Don't try to finish all the events of the day; that would be impossible. When the fifteen or twenty minutes is up, stop. This is the method of Pythagoras, who devoted his entire evening to meditating on the occurrences of the day.

For developing the power of auditory imagination the following methods are useful. Recall to mind the words and melody of some familiar song as rendered by a good singer, and imagine how it sounds. Hear the words, note the quality of the voice and accompaniment. Three or four songs or three or four repetitions of the same song are enough for once.

Call up in your memory one at a time the various sounds of the country and hear them in imagination— the hum of bees, the sound of the wind, the rustling leaves, the cries of the various birds, the lowing of cattle, and other noises peculiar to the life of the country.

Another exercise of value is the following: Recall some experience of your past which, at the time, made a strong impression upon you. Review it in all its details, slowly and carefully. Consider its causes, the means whereby it would have been prevented, outside influences which affected it, the consequences of the occurrence upon yourself and others. What influence has it had upon your life since that time? Good? Bad? Why? If good, may the same experience not be realized again? If bad, by what means may it be avoided? This method should be followed with various experiences. As you can easily understand, the exercise develops far more than imagination. It teaches reason, judgment, self-control, and that thoughtful intelligent care of the self which is the happy medium between brutal selfishness and base self-abnegation.

Another helpful exercise is the following: Recall some attractive landscape that you have seen. Paint from memory a picture of it: Suppose it was a running brook in the mountains. Remember the rocks at the shore, the trees with their low hanging branches, the cows that used to stand knee deep in the water at noon. Call to memory the twitter of birds in the foliage, the hoarse cawing of the crows in the not distant pines, the occasional lowing of a cow in the adjoining field. Hear the laughter of the boys as they come for an early evening plunge in the cool still water of the near-by mill pond.

Smell again in imagination the odor of the earth, the trees, the wild flowers, the fresh cut hay in the near-by meadow. Go through it all minutely, resolutely. Don't omit any detail.

Then begin on the creative phase of the imagination. Paint a picture in your mind, first, say a landscape—a view of a high mountain on the right, a great tree on the left, between the two a verdure clad hillside, beyond a lake, above a blue sky, low upon which hangs the setting sun. Add all the details which I have not space to enumerate.

Compose many pictures like this, taking time to put in every little bush and rock and cloud. Unless you make the picture vivid and complete, you will miss the real benefit of the exercise. Every picture ever painted has been thus elaborated in the imagination of the artist before it was objectified upon the canvas.

Next add action to your picture.

Upon the lake is a little sailboat containing a merry party. How many? How do they look? How are they dressed, etc.? Suddenly a squall comes up. The boat capsizes. Another boat puts out from shore and rescues the unfortunates. And so on.

One of the most interesting and valuable of exercises for the imagination is this: You are reading a book of fiction, and have reached, let us say, the end of the third chapter. Now sit down and write out of your own imagination a sequel to the story from the point at which you stopped reading. Who is going to marry whom? How is the villain to be punished? What is to become of the adventuress and so on. Write another sequel at the end of the fourth chapter. At the end of the fifth, the eighth, the tenth chapters do the same thing.

Now in this exercise, while the incidental literary practice is most valuable, the main point is to train the imagination. You should therefore think, imagine more than you write, setting out the rest of the story as you imagine it in brief simple terms and yet extended enough to be clear. Take much time. Better to work out one good, ingenious sequel in five hours than to spend twice that amount of time in doing hurried, blurred and incomplete work.

Lastly make up an entire story. Imagine your hero—if you like, a heroine. Develop your situation, and bring matters to a logical termination. It is best training for the mind (for all the other faculties as well as for the imagination) not to put the story into writing until it is completed in thought. Some of the most successful story writers follow this method, never committing the story to writing until it has been fully elaborated in the imagination. The best plan is to first block out in the imagination the general plot of the story. Then go over it again and again, elaborating the situations and adding details, until the whole story seems like an occurrence in your own personal experience.

Then write it out, making no special attempt at literary form, but striving only for clearness and exactness of description and detail. You may then make a second copy or even a third, if you like, with every writing trying to gain a more and more clear mental picture of the personages, scenes, and occurrences which make up your story.

A few hours a week devoted to study along lines which I have here sketched, will do wonders, not only in cultivating the power of imagination, but in developing every desirable quality of mind.

VII.

HOW TO CONCENTRATE THE ATTENTION.

Attention makes the genius.—WILL-MOT.

Genius is merely continued atten-tion.—HELVETIUS.

Attention is a sure mark of the supe-rior genius.—LORD CHESTERFIELD.

Attention is the stuff that memory is made of.—JAMES RUSSELL LOWELL.

If I have made any improvement in the sciences it is owing more to patient attention than to anything else.—SIR ISAAC NEWTON.

ONCENTRATION of the attention is one of the master keys of power. Without it one can accomplish nothing great or significant. The most perfect perceptions, the most retentive

99

memory, the most daring and picturesque imagination—without concentration they can effect nothing. The principle of concentration may be well illustrated by a physical comparison. Suppose we take a football weighing four ounces and propel it through the air by means of the charge of powder generally used for a projectile of four ounces' weight. What effect will the impact of the football have? None whatever. But suppose we concentrate the four ounces' weight into a sphere of lead less than half an inch in diameter and put behind it the same propulsive force—what then will happen? Now the difference between the football and the leaden bullet is the difference between diffusion and concentration—the difference between the impingement that is harmless and that which is deadly.

And so it is in the world of thought. The thoughts of some people are like a football—big, expanded by wordy wind, slow moving, ineffective; the thoughts of others are like bullets—concentrated, swift, direct, going straight to the center, without pause or hindrance.

"This one thing I do," said that profound philosopher, Paul of Tarsus. And if we study the history of the world's master spirits we shall find that this has been their policy. The uncouth butcher who pushed Charles I. from the throne and established a form of government based on moral principle instead of special right; the pallid, undersized French advocate who, in the hope of establishing his wild dream of democracy, sent the flower of French aristocracy walking up Dr. Guillotine's stairway; the ignorant tinker who gave to the world what is perhaps the greatest allegory in profane literature; the undersized plebeian Corsican adventurer, who made himself master of the world—all these had for their motto

101

the idea of concentration—"This one thing I do."

Now what is meant by concentration of the attention, or, as it is sometimes called, the power of attention? You see, in the kind of language which I am using to you, we do not attempt to express things with scientific precision; for that means the use not only of many, many words, but the introduction of many new, and to us, unnecessary words. So for our purpose we may use the terms, concentration, power of attention, concentration of attention, as if they meant the same thing—as they actually do.

WHAT IS CONCENTRATION?

Now what is concentration? In a word, concentration may be defined as being that state of mind in which the total and entire energies of the individual, physical as well as mental, are focused upon the thing he is doing or thinking. All actions and all thoughts not connected with what he is doing or thinking are kept out of the mind; and all his forces are bent upon the task in hand. He who can do this has concentration, has the power of attention. He who has not this power must acquire it before he can hope to do or be anything admirable or worthy in the world.

Any one who has performed any difficult feat of strength, such as lifting a heavy weight, "muscling" himself up on the horizontal bar or trying to make a track record at the "hundred yard dash" or the "two-twenty," will realize how large a factor in these muscular performances is the mere fact of concentration. In these, as well as in a great many other so-called physical feats, such as jumping, marksmanship, shot putting and so on, the slightest wandering of the mind from the work in hand is absolutely destructive of success. In acrobatic work, such as flying trapeze and flying rings, as well as in juggling and balancing, the same is true. Acrobatic jugglers and gymnasts are always masters of the art of attention—of concentration as applied to their special feats.

ATTENTION LARGELY A NEGATIVE ACT.

Now concentration is largely a negative process; it depends as much upon what you do not do, as upon what you do.

To take an example: You sit down to write a difficult letter. The trolley car whizzes by with its villainous "bang-bang." You are suddenly reminded that you should have gone down town to get that book your wife wanted. But there's the letter. You turn back to it. You write another line or two, and then—suddenly you hear the excited bark of little Fido, the Scotch terrier. You go to the window and look out. Nothing the matter—only another terrier not quite so Scotch across the street. You read back a few lines of your letter and start again. You don't quite know what to say. Your eye wanders round the room. Ah, yes, that suit to be pressed. You attend to this matter. Then back to your letter. And so on. A half hour has passed, and the letter is only begun. Now this is a fair example of the lack of concentration—of a wandering mind. And such a habit of thought is an absolute bar to any achievement that is helpful either to one's self or to the world at large.

And how shall this tendency be overcome? By what means may we gain the power of bringing every faculty of the mind to bear upon the task of the moment, without allowing any of our thought or attention to wander into other directions.

It is very simple—simple, but not at first easy. Merely refuse to let the mind wander. Be the master of your mind—of yourself. Remember what Milton says: "He who is master of

105

himself is king of men." But of course
you want more specific directions than
this. It is easy to say, "concentrate";
but you need to know exactly how to
concentrate.

Remembering that attention is
merely the act of applying the mind,
the entire mind, to the task in hand,
you will understand that the faithful
practice of the various exercises advised
in previous chapters of this series cannot but be of the greatest value as aids
to the development of the power of
attention. Every effort of the mind,
whether to perceive, to recollect, to
associate, to imagine, or to judge, must
necessarily involve a concentration of
the faculties of the mind upon that
particular act, whatever it may be.
So, first of all, I may assure you that
the practices I have advised, if you
have faithfully followed them, will
have by this time notably increased
your power of attention. As a matter
of fact, such assurance on my part is

superfluous; for if you have exercised
as I have directed, you, yourself, will
already have noted a marked change
in this direction as well as in others.

Do not allow yourself to overlook the
fact that whatever may be the mental
act in which you are engaged, the act
of attention is necessarily involved.
There is no faculty of the mind in
which you have so many opportunities
of exercise.

So the first exercise I shall advise is
that you go over carefully all the methods which I have detailed in the chapters
on perception, memory, association, imagination, and judgment, making a special effort while doing them not to allow
the mind to wander for a moment from
the task in hand. This alone, if persistently and conscientiously done,
would insure you a high degree of this
splendid intellectual accomplishment.

One of the best methods I know for
him or her who would begin at the

beginning and learn to concentrate the attention is the following:—

Select some task, which, while simple, requires accuracy and close attention. A sum in addition or multiplication is well adapted for this purpose. Now settle yourself down to this; resolving that, until it is finished and verified, you will not allow the mind to take in, or at any rate hold, any other idea or picture whatever.

While adding or multiplying the figures, you will suddenly find that there pops into the mind some other idea— the clang of a bell (fire or the ambulance); a shouting on the street (a fight or a runaway); a thought of the landlady, your tailor, your grocer.

Now just here is where you are required to make the essential act of concentration—of trained attention. Shut the door on these outside thoughts. Turn back to your work. For a time, at any rate, you cannot prevent the intrusion of extraneous thoughts; you can, however, resolutely refuse to allow them to remain in the mind. At first they will come, insistently, again and again, beating at the door of your consciousness. "Let me in; let me in," they cry. "Never mind those stupid figures. I am more interesting. I am more important to you. You must, you ought, you've got to think of me. Let me in." "But no," says the trained mind. "This one thing I do. One thing at a time. I can think of but one object at once; and if I let you into my mind I can do justice neither to you nor to my task. Avaunt." But the haunters do not retreat so easily. They return and return with incredible persistency. They pound at the door of your mind. They insist on intruding, and occasionally they get in.

Then—don't worry or fret about them. Don't let them bother or excite you. Don't be discouraged. Simply bring the attention back to the original subject of thought. As Dr. William

James, Professor of Psychology in Harvard, has said: "Effort of attention is the essential phenomenon of will."

Another exercise for concentration of the attention is simply to count. Count one hundred beginning with 2 and adding three each time, e. g., 2, 5, 8, 11, 14, etc. Or, beginning with 2, add 6, 7, 9, 13, or 17 each time, e. g., 2, 8, 14, 20, etc.; 2, 9, 16, 23, 30, etc.; 2, 11, 20, 29, 38, etc. Or, beginning with 100, count downward, subtracting 3, 6, 7, 9, 11, 13, 17, or 19 each time, e. g., 100, 97, 94, 91, etc. All this may seem very simple. But you will find that, unless you already have a very finely developed power of attention, you will not at first be able to complete the hundred in any of these exercises without the entrance into the mind of vagrant, extraneous thoughts. By the time you are able to add or subtract freely in this way without any wandering of the attention, you may congratulate yourself on having acquired to an unusual degree the power of concentrated attention.

For the next exercise you will need about three dozen large sized blank cards: the best size is about three by five inches. Upon one of these cards write a number of four figures, such as 4357. Upon several others write four figures arranged in a square, as 47 and under that 93. Then on several cards write six figures, as 457, under which you place 236, or figures such as 47, 52, and 96 under each other. Other cards should contain from seven to ten numbers in a simple column.

Prepare a dozen of these cards. Now to use them: Shuffle the cards, face downward. Draw one, give a rapid glance at its face, and then repeat aloud the numbers that you saw, first in the order in which they were written, i. e., 4357, then backward, 7534. Or, to take another card, repeat 47, 52, 96, in the order in which they appear. Then backward, 96, 52, 47; then go down the units column, 7, 2, 6, then up the tens column, 9, 5, 4, and so on.

After a few hours of practice such as this, you will begin to know the figures on each card by memory. This, while a good thing in one way, makes the exercise of less value as a training in concentration; so it will be necessary for you to make up another set. In the second set make a larger number of figures on each card, say something like 947, 853, 201, under each other, making a square of nine figures, or 94, 78, 53, 20, 16 in a column, or a line of twelve or fifteen single figures, arranged as for an example in addition.

After a period of practice with these cards you will find again that you are learning to remember the numbers from previous glances rather than from the one last glance. Then it is time to make another set. This time make

your figure squares still larger. Run
them up to squares like this: 4702,
3895, 6374, 9765, etc.; or make collections of numbers like 470, 238, 956,
etc., making a list of perhaps five or
six lines of three figures each. In my
own experience along this line I have
known of students who could remember with unerring fidelity a figure
square consisting of sixty-four figures
arranged in a square, as 48964325,
93842739, etc. It seems incredible;
but it is entirely true that, after a
time, it is quite as easy to recall a
mental picture of sixty-four figures as
of twelve or sixteen.

It is perhaps an improvement on the
above described practice to have the
assistance of another who will shuffle
the cards and exhibit one for a fleeting
second. Where you can get some one
to work with you, it is a good plan for
the assistant to read a few lines of
prose—say about twenty words at first
—which you afterwards repeat from

memory. Or he may call out a list of words or figures to which you listen and which you afterward repeat.

And now for the last and most important exercise which I have to suggest. And I may say right here that if you practice persistently and conscientiously you will acquire the power of concentration to a greater degree and in a shorter time than by all other methods combined. This exercise, like most things that are great and important, is also very simple. It is this: Make every detail a work of art. Think this over. It means that you do everything—the most trivial acts— with strict and exclusive attention.

Are you lacing your boots? There is a way in which that homely little act can be performed more rapidly, easily, and satisfactorily than it can in any other way. Standing, walking, dressing one's self, writing, shaking hands, shaving, handling knife and fork, opening a book—all these and a million other trivial acts—if done consciously and attentively, afford a training in concentration which it is absolutely impossible to gain in any other way. When asked by some inquisitive reporter the secret of his success, "Sunset" Cox replied: "I think it is my attention to detail. I pride myself upon the way I can wrap up a paper parcel." This is the true spirit—"the pride of success." Make every detail a work of art.

And then the gain! You develop not only the power of concentration. You develop perception, memory, association, imagination, will. And this is one of the most satisfactory results of the practice of mental training—in developing any one faculty you are at the same time developing others. But as regards concentration, when you are training that, you are at the same time training all the other powers of the mind.

VIII.

PSYCHO-PHYSICAL DEVELOP-MENT.

HE human body is one—
an entity. In ordinary
conversation we refer to
the individual as if he or
she were composed of
three different elements,
the physical, the mental, and the spiritual. In reality, however, these three are
merely different phases of one form
of activity. The spirit is the great
omniscient, omnipotent, omnipresent,
eternal thing which animates both
mind and body. Mind and body in
turn are merely representations of the
action of the spirit. In the perfectly
organized individual spirit, mind, and
body would act together perfectly without friction, without effort, without
the necessity for any special training.

117

There are, in fact, a few exceptional cases in which spirit, mind, and body act with some degree of harmony—in which the pure impersonal spirit (the Sat, the Atman, as the wise Hindoos call it) acts in such a manner as to largely dominate the thoughts, feelings, and movements of the individual. These people we call geniuses—the shining ones of the ages.

This intimate interaction of body, mind, and spirit is the mystic "at-one-ment" so frequently referred to in the writings of the old philosophers, Egyptian, Hindoo, Chinese, and Hebraic. Such harmonious action once achieved, the individual is in immediate possession of health, strength, energy, beauty, and expressiveness

As Browning writes in "Paracelsus":—

"There is an inmost centre in us all,
  Where truth abides in fullness; and
      to know

Rather consists in opening out a way
Whence the imprisoned splendor may
     escape,
Than in effecting entry for a light
Supposed to be without."

A wiser teacher than Browning said: "Seek ye first the Kingdom of Heaven and His righteousness; and all these things shall be added unto you." The Kingdom of Heaven as used in this and other cases by Jesus undoubtedly refers to this mystic "at-one-ment" between spirit, mind, and body. "As a man thinketh in his heart so is he."

Two Phases of Human Action.

In every human action there are two distinct phases—thought and motion. Thoughts lie hidden in the gray caverns of the brain. They are potential, latent. Motions are physical, obvious. Every thought, every impulse, every emotion has its ellipsis in some action of the muscles; and when such thought, impulse, or emotion is perfectly expressed in muscular activity, we have the ideal human being. In this connection it may be appropriate to introduce two brief quotations from the writings of Professor William James of Harvard College.

He says: "There is no more valuable precept in moral education than this—if we wish to conquer undesirable emotional tendencies in ourselves, we must assiduously, and in the first instance cold-bloodedly, go through the outward movements of those contrary dispositions we prefer to cultivate. . . . . Smooth the brow, brighten the eye, contract the dorsal rather than the ventral aspect of the frame, and speak in the major key, pass the genial compliment and your heart must be frigid indeed if it does not gradually thaw."

And in another place the same author has said: "No reception without reaction, no impression without correlative expression,—this is the great

maxim which the teacher ought never
to forget. An impression which simply flows in at the pupil's eyes or ears,
and in no way modifies the active life,
is an impression gone to waste. It is
physiologically incomplete. It leaves
no fruits behind it in the way of capac-
ity acquired. Even as mere impression it fails to produce its proper effect
upon the memory; for to remain fully
among the acquisitions of this latter
faculty, it must be wrought into the
whole cycle of our operations. Its
motor consequences are what clinch it.
Some effect, due to it in the way of
activity, must return to the mind in
the form of the sensation of having
acted, and connect itself with the impression. The most durable impressions, in fact, are those on account of
which we speak or act, or else are in-
wardly convulsed."

Of all the many evil effects of what
we call civilization, the most blasting is
that its general influence is to break up

the close interrelation between thought and motion. In order to live the conventional life of the well-behaved man or woman one is compelled to constantly stifle and deny desires, impulses, thoughts, and such denial inevitably leads to injury of mind and body.

RELATION OF MIND AND BODY.

Mental activity simply means certain chemical and mechanical changes occurring in nervous matter. These changes occur not only in the nervous matter of the brain, but also in the nerves which cause muscular action.

This is a large subject and it is quite impossible within the limits of a work such as this to make it clear. It may be said at once, however, that each emotion and each thought has its corresponding output along the motor nerves—that each emotion and each thought has a muscular picture which is peculiar to itself. Now, if the muscles be free and flexible, the thought which occupies the higher nerve centers will be translated by a certain position of the muscles. In other words, a person marked by such peculiarity will be expressive and interesting. All the great singers, actors, and orators—all those most successful on the stage, in politics or in society— have been distinguished by this peculiar expressiveness.

In order to be expressive several things are requisite. The body must be erect, the joints and hinges of the body, as explained in previous chapters, being each in its proper place. There must have been acquired the habit of keeping the muscles in a state of relaxation and receptivity. Among the many exercises which the writer has employed for the purpose of developing this power are the few given herewith. A careful study and practice of these exercises can hardly fail to result in an increase in general expressiveness, health, and personality.

Exercise No. 1.

(Anticipation, pleasurable expectation.)

Imagine that some one is coming toward you whom you very much wished to see. You would naturally lean forward to greet him, extending one or both hands and smiling. Now, holding this idea, this mental picture, before the mind, allow the flexible body to show it forth in gesture, facial expression, and a few words of greeting spoken aloud. Exactly what you do does not in the least matter. Simply hold the thought so intently that for the moment you accept the imagined situation as real, and let the body go.

This exercise may be varied infinitely by changing the picture, always, however, imagining a situation such as will produce a feeling of pleasurable anticipation.

Exercise No. 2.

(Horror.)

Imagine that you are looking at some dangerous animal (a snake, if you are a man: if a woman, a mouse will answer every purpose) that you cannot escape. You naturally draw back in horror.

Like the former exercise, in this you are to forget the body entirely—to let it go—putting all your attention upon the imagined situation. In this exercise, as in the preceding, any situation may be invented which will induce the thought of horror.

Exercise No. 3.

(Joy.)

Imagine some situation which would awaken in you a state of joy and yield the body up to the feeling.

Exercise No. 4.

(Guilt.)

Try to imagine that you have committed some crime, say, for instance, theft. Imagine that you are brought before a judge and that you are pleading guilty and asking for mercy. Allow this thought to permeate mind and body, showing by gestures and attitude your appreciation of the situation.

Exercise No. 5.

(Accusation.)

Imagine that some one has committed a crime against you; that you are facing him before a tribunal. Make your accusation, if necessary, in words, taking at the same time the attitude appropriate to this emotional state.

Exercise No. 6.

(Depression.)

Imagine such circumstances as would produce in you a feeling of depression and yield the body to it.

These exercises, although they may seem unusual, have powerful and far-reaching results. That this is true any one may prove to himself in a week of faithful practice. It must be understood, however, that they cannot be properly practiced until the body has been made erect and thoroughly flexible by a persevering practice of the exercises described in preceding chapters.

As to mental images, literature and poetry afford many suggestions. David at the bier of Absalom, Hero over the body of Leander, Socrates drinking the cup of hemlock, Luther on the way to Worms, Hamlet before his father's ghost, Robinson Crusoe when he discovers the footprint in the sand, Rip

127

Van Winkle on awakening from his long sleep, Mark Antony in his speech to the Romans, Regulus parting from his wife and children—these and many other scenes afford vivid dramatic situations.

In all this work the great point is to subordinate the body, to make the body obedient, flexible, acquiescent, and interpretative of the mind. Those who are interested in any form of expressive art, dramatic, lyrical, or scenic, will find these simple exercises of value.

IX.

THE LOST ARTS OF CHILDHOOD.

Except ye be converted and become as little children ye shall not enter into the kingdom of heaven.—MATTHEW 18, 3.

For of such is the kingdom of heaven. —MATTHEW 19, 14.

THE more deeply the man of science studies the sayings attributed to Jesus, the Seer of Judea, the more profoundly is he impressed not only by the brilliant intellect and wonderful oratory of Jesus, but by his marvelous insight into subjects which were in his time unknown even to the most lucid thinkers of ancient times.

In the history of the race two thousand years is not a very long time, and previous to the beginning of the Christian era there had been accomplished along lines of philosophical, physical, and cosmological research much more than, with all our boasted erudition, has been done since. In fact, some of our most striking discoveries are merely corroborations of knowledge of the Brahmins, the Chinese, the Phœnicians, and other of the ancient peoples who lived thousands of years before the alleged appearance of Jesus of Nazareth.

How much of this ancient knowledge Jesus possessed it is impossible to say—probably most if not all. One thing is certain: Some things he knew and said, which, so far as we know, were entirely original and iconoclastic. And one of these things, entirely new then (and almost entirely new now, for that matter) was to the effect that in child study we should find the key to the kingdom of heaven.

Now as I have explained elsewhere

in these Sermons of a Scientist, the Kingdom of Heaven (or the Kingdom of God) is not a place where good people go when they die. The Kingdom of Heaven is a state of mind, of Spirit —that state in which spirit, therefore mind, therefore body, are all three in harmony with the Great Oversoul, and with His laws.

For us who are adults, who for three, four, or five decades have been guilty of the thousand, thousand crimes, physical, mental, spiritual, incidental to commonplace living—for us it is necessary to be reborn to be radically changed in spirit, therefore in mind and body, before we can enter the Kingdom of Heaven, the physical realm of peace, rest, and power. So Jesus said to the disciples: "Verily I say unto you, except ye be converted and become as little children, ye shall not enter into the Kingdom of Heaven." By which He meant exactly what He did when He said to Nicodemus: "Ex-

131

cept a man be born again, he cannot
see the Kingdom of God."

Of the many millions that have, with
close attention and deep reverence, read
the words I have quoted, few, if any,
have seen the clear, profound, practical wisdom of the statement of Jesus
that only the man, the woman, who
became as a little child, could enter into
the realm of peace and power.

And now let us analyze a little.
What is there about the child which we
should emulate? What characteristics
has the child, unpossessed by the adult
which when developed in the adult will
give entrance into the kingdom of God?

Mind you, it is not stated that children are in the Kingdom of Heaven.
Nor can they be. They lack the actual
knowledge, the experience, the poise.
But it is in the experience, the hard
and bitter experience which develops
poise and power, that man loses the
simplicity, trustfulness, and tenderness
of childhood. It is when, in addition

132

to his adult powers, he achieves the lost arts and powers of childhood, that he enters the Kingdom of Heaven.

WHAT ARE THE LOST ARTS OF CHILDHOOD?

Let us consider first some of the physical characteristics of normal childhood. The healthy child is remarkable for his erect body, his upturned face, his clear and far-reaching voice, the ease and grace of his movements, his wonderful endurance. That these are among the normal powers of the average healthy child may be determined by a few minutes of close observation upon any playground. A moment's thought will show how rare are such powers among adults.

The healthy child is erect. Therefore the chest is high and expanded, the body is carried like an erect column and the breathing is slow and deep. This gives the only conditions under which the normal tone of voice in song or speech can be reproduced. The erect carriage means that the joints and muscles of the body are in their normal and mechanical relation to each other.

So we have in the normal child movements which are at once rapid, graceful, and economical—so economical of vital force that the child's endurance has passed into a proverb. Children will keep on romping for hours at a time without fatigue. But an adult who joins in their play will usually be tired out in ten or fifteen minutes. Why is this? Because the child moves properly and the adult does not move properly. Because bodily movement is one of the lost arts of childhood.

A MASTER OF THE DIFFICULT ART OF REST.

And then the ability to rest. The tired child throws himself down on the couch or floor or ground and rests. The tired adult, on the other hand,

134

often fidgets, tosses, fumes, and worries because he can't sleep. Then his sleep, when it comes, is not restful; and he awakens after eight or more hours quite as fatigued as when he went to bed. Few adults have retained from childhood the power to rest. For the power to rest is another one of the lost arts of childhood; and he who would enter the Kingdom of Heaven, the realm of peace, must be a master of the difficult art of rest.

The world is full of men and women whose most ardent ambition is to succeed in some art—music, painting, acting, writing. And out of the multitude who drudge laboriously, unrestingly at their chosen task how few succeed?

But—study the little children. Watch them at play, when they believe themselves unobserved. They are playing "house," "school," "church," and so on. On no stage in the world will you find acting so true, so finished, so perfect an exposition of the actor's conception of his part. From a purely technical standpoint, the dramatic work of the average healthy, intelligent child is beyond criticism—it is simply perfect.

And then the child's moral and spiritual qualities. By nature he is absolutely truthful—truthful both in the sense of seeing the truth and of telling it—until he is seduced into lying by fear and bad example.

Michelet, that deep and tender philosopher, has said: "No consecrated absurdity of mankind would have survived one generation had not the man silenced the objection of the child."

Do you remember the first lies they told you? How strange it seemed for people, people whom perhaps you loved and feared and worshiped with the pure, white hot intensity of the child— how strange for them to do that!

Soon, however, you learned to do it yourself, learned the fatal utility, the convenience of the lie. And so the angel with the flaming sword waved you away from the Eden of Unconquerable Innocence, and only after many years of wandering in waste places, only by being born again, may you re-enter Eden, the Kingdom of Heaven.

And, with the truthfulness of childhood, the simplicity, the kindliness, the democracy, the independence—all of these are among the lost powers of childhood and all of these we must achieve if we would possess the highest powers of body, mind, and spirit.

"Except ye become as a little child" no true power, physical, artistic, intellectual, spiritual, is possible. To him or her who in simplicity accepts the teaching, the kingdom is close at hand; and "a little child shall lead them." The truly great of earth are not the ones most highly polished by conventional educational methods. On the other hand, they are often the lonely and the neglected. They have starved in garrets and dreamed in hovels; from squalid prison cells they have sent forth "thoughts that breathe"; under the silent stars they have conceived thoughts as high as the stars themselves. They are those who "through great tribulation" have been born again, and who, as little children, have entered into the realm of peace, wisdom, love, and power, the mystic Kingdom of Heaven.

THE NAUTILUS

is a monthly efficiency tonic for mind, body, and business. It is recognized as the leading magazine of the New Thought and mental healing movement. It deals dynamically with practical subjects connected with everyday living.

ITS EDITOR is ELIZABETH TOWNE, whose editorials, which are part of the magazine monthly, are said to have the largest number of readers of any woman's writings in America, with one possible exception.

ITS REGULAR CONTRIBUTORS include Edwin Markham, Orison Swett Marden, Dr. Edward B. Warman, William Walker Atkinson, Horatio W. Dresser, Thomas Dreier, and many others.

Each number of *Nautilus* contains two or three beautiful original poems.

ITS DEPARTMENTS are contributions to and from its readers. They are of remarkable interest. In "Things That Make For Success," a monthly prize is offered to subscribers for the best letter on success, and every six months $5.00 in cash is given to the author of the best success letter published during that period. In "Family Counsel," the most popular department, Elizabeth Towne answers questions from subscribers.

NAUTILUS is handsomely printed, covers in two colors, illustrated with original drawings and half-tones. Subscription, $1.50 per year. Address,

THE ELIZABETH TOWNE CO.,
HOLYOKE, MASS.

CPSIA information can be obtained
at www.ICGtesting.com
Printed in the USA
BVHW011651130620
581343BV00014B/296